Wiggly Croc
DISHCLOTHS ™

Contents

Concentric Squares

SKILL LEVEL

INTERMEDIATE

FINISHED SIZE

10½ inches x 11 inches

MATERIALS
- Omega Sinfonia light (light worsted) weight yarn (3½ oz/218 yds/100g per ball):
    1 ball each #820 bright yellow, #879 purple, #823 garnet and #880 green
- Size F/5/3.75mm crochet hook or size needed to obtain gauge
- Tapestry needle

GAUGE

3 meshes = 1¾ inches; 4 mesh rows = 2½ inches

Take time to check gauge.

PATTERN NOTES

Weave in ends as work progresses.

Join with slip stitch as indicated unless otherwise stated.

Chain-2 at beginning of round counts as first half double crochet unless otherwise stated.

Chain-5 at beginning of row counts as first extended double crochet and chain-2 sp unless otherwise stated.

SPECIAL STITCHES

Mesh: Ch 2, sk next 2 chs, extended dc in next ch or st.

Extended double crochet (extended dc): Yo, insert hook in indicated st, yo, pull up lp, yo, pull through 1 lp on hook, [yo, pull through 2 lps on hook] twice.

DISHCLOTH
FOUNDATION MESH

Row 1 (RS): With bright yellow, ch 57, **extended dc** (*see Special Stitches*) in 9th ch from hook (*first mesh*), **mesh** (*see Special Stitches*) across, turn. (*17 mesh*)

Row 2: Ch 5 (*see Pattern Notes*), sk next 2 chs, extended dc in next st, mesh across, turn.

COLOR KEY
■ Purple
■ Garnet
■ Green

Rows 3–17: Rep row 2. At end of last row, fasten off.

WIGGLY CROCHET

Rnd 1: With RS facing, **join** (*see Pattern Notes*) purple in last mesh on row 17 at dot on Chart in top left corner, **ch 2** (*see Pattern Notes*), 2 hdc in same mesh, working 3 hdc around each extended dc post and in each ch-2 sp of mesh, follow path on Chart around to beg with 6 hdc in each corner ch-5 sp, join in 2nd ch of beg ch-2. Fasten off.

Rnd 2: With garnet, work next square in same manner, beg at dot on Chart and following path around to beg, join in 2nd ch of beg ch-2. Fasten off.

Next rnds: Work other sections in same manner, beg at each dot on Chart and following path around to beg, join in 2nd ch of beg ch-2. Fasten off. ■

Concentric Squares
Chart

Crosses & Dots

SKILL LEVEL

INTERMEDIATE

FINISHED SIZE

10½ inches x 10½ inches

MATERIALS

- Omega Sinfonia light (light worsted) weight yarn (3½ oz/218 yds/100g per ball):
  1 ball each #801 white, #816 teal, #842 cinnamon and #862 wheat
- Size F/5/3.75mm crochet hook or size needed to obtain gauge
- Tapestry needle

GAUGE
3 meshes = 1¾ inches; 4 mesh rows = 2½ inches

Take time to check gauge.

PATTERN NOTES
Weave in ends as work progresses.

Join with slip stitch as indicated unless otherwise stated.

Chain-2 at beginning of round counts as first half double crochet unless otherwise stated.

Chain-5 at beginning of row counts as first extended double crochet and chain-2 sp unless otherwise stated.

SPECIAL STITCHES
Mesh: Ch 2, sk next 2 chs, extended dc in next ch or st.

Extended double crochet (extended dc): Yo, insert hook in indicated st, yo, pull up lp, yo, pull through 1 lp on hook, [yo, pull through 2 lps on hook] twice.

DISHCLOTH
FOUNDATION MESH
Row 1 (RS): With white, ch 57, **extended dc** (*see Special Stitches*) in 9th ch from hook (*first mesh*), **mesh** (*see Special Stitches*) across, turn. (*17 mesh*)

Row 2: **Ch 5** (*see Pattern Notes*), sk next 2 chs, extended dc in next st, mesh across, turn.

Rows 3–17: Rep row 2. At end of last row, fasten off.

WIGGLY CROCHET
Rnd 1: With RS facing, **join** (*see Pattern Notes*) teal in last mesh on row 17 at dot on Chart in top left corner, **ch 2** (*see Pattern Notes*), 2 hdc in same mesh, working 3 hdc around each dc post and in each ch-2 sp of mesh, follow path on Chart around to beg with 6 hdc in each corner ch-5 sp, join in 2nd ch of beg ch-2. Fasten off.

Next rnds: With cinnamon, work crosses in same manner, beg at dot on Chart and following path around to beg, join in 2nd ch of beg ch-2. Fasten off.

Next rnds: With wheat, work circles in same manner, beg at each dot on Chart and following path around to beg, join in 2nd ch of beg ch-2. Fasten off. ∎

COLOR KEY
- Teal
- Cinnamon
- Wheat

Crosses & Dots
Chart

Diagonals

SKILL LEVEL

INTERMEDIATE

FINISHED SIZE
12 inches x 12 inches

MATERIALS

- Omega Sinfonia light (light worsted) weight yarn (3½ oz/218 yds/100g per ball):
   1 ball each #861 sand, #818 prairie green, #837 dark magenta, #824 burgundy and #869 gold
- Size F/5/3.75mm crochet hook or size needed to obtain gauge
- Tapestry needle

GAUGE
3 meshes = 1¾ inches; 4 mesh rows = 2½ inches

Take time to check gauge.

PATTERN NOTES
Weave in ends as work progresses.

Join with slip stitch as indicated unless otherwise stated.

Chain-2 at beginning of round counts as first half double crochet unless otherwise stated.

Chain-5 at beginning of row counts as first extended double crochet and chain-2 sp unless otherwise stated.

SPECIAL STITCHES
Mesh: Ch 2, sk next 2 chs, extended dc in next ch or st.

Extended double crochet (extended dc): Yo, insert hook in indicated st, yo, pull up lp, yo, pull through 1 lp on hook, [yo, pull through 2 lps on hook] twice.

DISHCLOTH
FOUNDATION MESH
Row 1 (RS): With sand, ch 63, **extended dc** (see Special Stitches) in 9th ch from hook (first mesh), **mesh** (see Special Stitches) across, turn. (19 mesh)

Row 2: Ch 5 (see Pattern Notes), sk next 2 chs, extended dc in next st, mesh across, turn.

COLOR KEY
- ▦ Prairie green
- ▪ Dark magenta
- ▪ Burgundy
- ☐ Gold

Rows 3–19: Rep row 2. At end of last row, fasten off.

WIGGLY CROCHET
Rnd 1: With RS facing, **join** (see Pattern Notes) prairie green in last mesh on row 19 at dot on Chart in top left corner, **ch 2** (see Pattern Notes), 2 hdc in same mesh, working 3 hdc around each extended dc post and in each ch-2 sp of mesh, follow path on Chart around to beg with 6 hdc in each corner ch-5 sp, join in 2nd ch of beg ch-2. Fasten off.

Rnd 2: With dark magenta, work larger diamond in center area in same manner, beg at dot on Chart and following path around to beg, join in 2nd ch of beg ch-2. Fasten off.

Next rnds: Work other sections in same manner, beg at each dot on Chart and following path around to beg, join in 2nd ch of beg ch-2. Fasten off. ∎

Diagonals
Chart

Nine Squares

SKILL LEVEL

INTERMEDIATE

FINISHED SIZE
12 inches x 12½ inches

MATERIALS
- Omega Sinfonia light (light worsted) weight yarn (3½ oz/218 yds/100g per ball):
    1 ball each #801 white, #865 blue orchid, #883 coral, #868 sandstone and #819 light olive
- Size F/5/3.75mm crochet hook or size needed to obtain gauge
- Tapestry needle

GAUGE
3 meshes = 1¾ inches; 4 mesh rows = 2½ inches

Take time to check gauge.

PATTERN NOTES
Weave in ends as work progresses.

Join with slip stitch as indicated unless otherwise stated.

Chain-2 at beginning of round counts as first half double crochet unless otherwise stated.

Chain-5 at beginning of row counts as first extended double crochet and chain-2 sp unless otherwise stated.

SPECIAL STITCHES
Mesh: Ch 2, sk next 2 chs, extended dc in next ch or st.

Extended double crochet (extended dc): Yo, insert hook in indicated st, yo, pull up lp, yo, pull through 1 lp on hook, [yo, pull through 2 lps on hook] twice.

DISHCLOTH
FOUNDATION MESH
Row 1 (RS): With white, ch 63, **extended dc** (see Special Stitches) in 9th ch from hook (first mesh), **mesh** (see Special Stitches) across, turn. (19 mesh)

Row 2: **Ch 5** (see Pattern Notes), sk next 2 chs, extended dc in next st, mesh across, turn.

COLOR KEY
■ Blue orchid
■ Coral
□ Sandstone
■ Light olive

Rows 3–19: Rep row 2. At end of last row, fasten off.

WIGGLY CROCHET
Rnd 1: With RS facing, **join** (see Pattern Notes) blue orchid in last mesh on row 19 at dot on Chart in top left corner, **ch 2** (see Pattern Notes), 2 hdc in same mesh, working 3 hdc around each extended dc post and in each ch-2 sp of mesh, follow path on Chart around to beg with 6 hdc in each corner ch-5 sp, join in 2nd ch of beg ch-2. Fasten off.

Rnd 2: With coral, work top right-hand corner square in same manner, beg at dot on Chart and following path around to beg, join in 2nd ch of beg ch-2. Fasten off.

Next rnds: Work other sections in same manner, beg at each dot on Chart and following path around to beg, join in 2nd ch of beg ch-2. Fasten off. ■

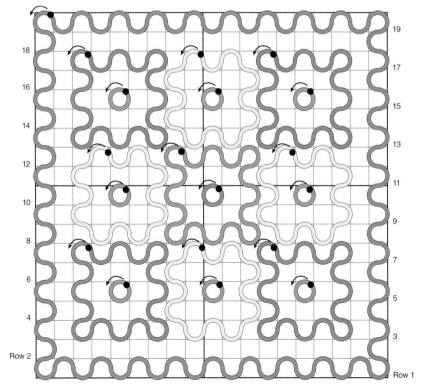

Nine Squares
Chart

Four **Squares**

SKILL LEVEL

INTERMEDIATE

FINISHED SIZE
12 inches x 12 inches

MATERIALS
- Omega Sinfonia light (light worsted) weight yarn (3½ oz/218 yds/100g per ball):
  1 ball each #801 white, #811 rose, #818 prairie green and #863 camel
- Size F/5/3.75mm crochet hook or size needed to obtain gauge
- Tapestry needle

GAUGE
3 meshes = 1¾ inches; 4 mesh rows = 2½ inches

Take time to check gauge.

PATTERN NOTES
Weave in ends as work progresses.

Join with slip stitch as indicated unless otherwise stated.

Chain-2 at beginning of round counts as first half double crochet unless otherwise stated.

Chain-5 at beginning of row counts as first extended double crochet and chain-2 sp unless otherwise stated.

SPECIAL STITCHES
Mesh: Ch 2, sk next 2 chs, extended dc in next ch or st.

Extended double crochet (extended dc): Yo, insert hook in indicated st, yo, pull up lp, yo, pull through 1 lp on hook, [yo, pull through 2 lps on hook] twice.

DISHCLOTH
FOUNDATION MESH
Row 1 (RS): With white, ch 63, **extended dc** *(see Special Stitches)* in 9th ch from hook *(first mesh)*, **mesh** *(see Special Stitches)* across, turn. *(19 mesh)*

Row 2: **Ch 5** *(see Pattern Notes)*, sk next 2 chs, extended dc in next st, mesh across, turn.

Rows 3–19: Rep row 2. At end of last row, fasten off.

WIGGLY CROCHET
Rnd 1: With RS facing, **join** *(see Pattern Notes)* rose in last mesh on row 19 at dot on Chart in top left corner, **ch 2** *(see Pattern Notes)*, 2 hdc in same mesh, working 3 hdc around each extended dc post and in each ch-2 sp of mesh, follow path on Chart around to beg with 6 hdc in corner ch sp, join in 2nd ch of beg ch-2. Fasten off.

Rnd 2: With prairie green, work top right-hand corner square in same manner, beg at dot on Chart and following path around to beg, working 6 hdc in corner ch-5 sp, join in 2nd ch of beg ch-2. Fasten off.

Next rnds: Work other sections in same manner, beg at each dot on Chart and following path around to beg, join in 2nd ch of beg ch-2. Fasten off. ∎

COLOR KEY	
■	Rose
■	Prairie green
☐	Camel

Four Squares
Chart

X's

SKILL LEVEL

INTERMEDIATE

FINISHED SIZE
12 inches x 12 inches

MATERIALS
- Omega Sinfonia light (light worsted) weight yarn (3½ oz/218 yds/100g per ball):
  1 ball each #801 white, #832 soft blue, #826 sky blue, #820 bright yellow and #867 baby yellow
- Size F/5/3.75mm crochet hook or size needed to obtain gauge
- Tapestry needle

GAUGE

3 meshes = 1¾ inches; 4 mesh rows = 2½ inches

Take time to check gauge.

PATTERN NOTES

Weave in ends as work progresses.

Join with slip stitch as indicated unless other-wise stated.

Chain-2 at beginning of round counts as first half double crochet unless otherwise stated.

Chain-5 at beginning of row counts as first extended double crochet and chain-2 sp unless otherwise stated.

SPECIAL STITCHES

Mesh: Ch 2, sk next 2 chs, extended dc in next ch or st.

Extended double crochet (extended dc): Yo, insert hook in indicated st, yo, pull up lp, yo, pull through 1 lp on hook, [yo, pull through 2 lps on hook] twice.

DISHCLOTH
FOUNDATION MESH

Row 1 (RS): With white, ch 63, **extended dc** *(see Special Stitches)* in 9th ch from hook *(first mesh)*, **mesh** *(see Special Stitches)* across, turn. *(19 mesh)*

Row 2: Ch 5 *(see Pattern Notes)*, sk next 2 chs, extended dc in next st, mesh across, turn.

COLOR KEY
■ Soft blue
■ Sky blue
□ Bright yellow
□ Baby yellow

Rows 3–19: Rep row 2. At end of last row, fasten off.

WIGGLY CROCHET

Rnd 1: With RS facing, **join** *(see Pattern Notes)* soft blue in last mesh on row 19 at dot on Chart in top left corner, **ch 2** *(see Pattern Notes)*, 2 hdc in same mesh, working 3 hdc around each extended dc post and in each ch-2 sp of mesh, follow path on Chart around to beg with 6 hdc in each corner ch-5 sp, join in 2nd ch of beg ch-2. Fasten off.

Rnd 2: With bright yellow, work center "X" in same manner, beg at dot on Chart and following path around to beg, join in 2nd ch of beg ch-2. Fasten off.

Next rnds: Work other sections in same manner, beg at each dot on Chart and following path around to beg, join in 2nd ch of beg ch-2. Fasten off. ■

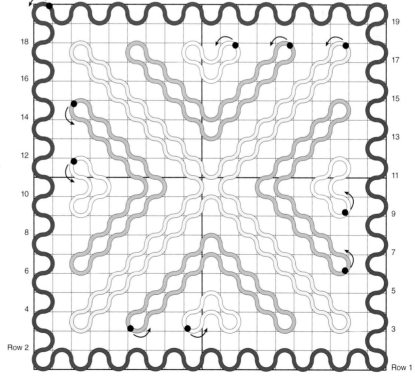

X's
Chart

Metric
Conversion
Charts

METRIC CONVERSIONS

yards	x	.9144	=	metres (m)
yards	x	91.44	=	centimetres (cm)
inches	x	2.54	=	centimetres (cm)
inches	x	25.40	=	millimetres (mm)
inches	x	.0254	=	metres (m)

centimetres	x	.3937	=	inches
metres	x	1.0936	=	yards

INCHES INTO MILLIMETRES & CENTIMETRES (Rounded off slightly)

inches	mm	cm	inches	cm	inches	cm	inches	cm
1/8	3	0.3	5	12.5	21	53.5	38	96.5
1/4	6	0.6	5 1/2	14	22	56	39	99
3/8	10	1	6	15	23	58.5	40	101.5
1/2	13	1.3	7	18	24	61	41	104
5/8	15	1.5	8	20.5	25	63.5	42	106.5
3/4	20	2	9	23	26	66	43	109
7/8	22	2.2	10	25.5	27	68.5	44	112
1	25	2.5	11	28	28	71	45	114.5
1 1/4	32	3.2	12	30.5	29	73.5	46	117
1 1/2	38	3.8	13	33	30	76	47	119.5
1 3/4	45	4.5	14	35.5	31	79	48	122
2	50	5	15	38	32	81.5	49	124.5
2 1/2	65	6.5	16	40.5	33	84	50	127
3	75	7.5	17	43	34	86.5		
3 1/2	90	9	18	46	35	89		
4	100	10	19	48.5	36	91.5		
4 1/2	115	11.5	20	51	37	94		

KNITTING NEEDLES CONVERSION CHART

Canada/U.S.	0	1	2	3	4	5	6	7	8	9	10	10½	11	13	15
Metric (mm)	2	2¼	2¾	3¼	3½	3¾	4	4½	5	5½	6	6½	8	9	10

CROCHET HOOKS CONVERSION CHART

Canada/U.S.	1/B	2/C	3/D	4/E	5/F	6/G	8/H	9/I	10/J	10½/K	N
Metric (mm)	2.25	2.75	3.25	3.5	3.75	4.25	5	5.5	6	6.5	9.0

STITCH GUIDE

FOR MORE COMPLETE INFORMATION,
VISIT **ANNIESCATALOG.COM/STITCHGUIDE**

STITCH ABBREVIATIONS

beg .... begin/begins/beginning
bpdc .... back post double crochet
bpsc .... back post single crochet
bptr .... back post treble crochet
CC .... contrasting color
ch(s) .... chain(s)
ch- .... refers to chain or space
previously made (i.e., ch-1 space)
ch sp(s) .... chain space(s)
cl(s) .... cluster(s)
cm .... centimeter(s)
dc .... double crochet (singular/plural)
dc dec .... double crochet 2 or more
stitches together, as indicated
dec .... decrease/decreases/decreasing
dtr .... double treble crochet
ext ....extended
fpdc .... front post double crochet
fpsc .... front post single crochet
fptr .... front post treble crochet
g .... gram(s)
hdc .... half double crochet
hdc dec .... half double crochet 2 or more
stitches together, as indicated
inc .... increase/increases/increasing
lp(s) .... loop(s)
MC .... main color
mm .... millimeter(s)
oz .... ounce(s)
pc .... popcorn(s)
rem .... remain/remains/remaining
rep(s) .... repeat(s)
rnd(s) .... round(s)
RS .... right side
sc .... single crochet (singular/plural)
sc dec .... single crochet 2 or more
stitches together, as indicated
sk .... skip/skipped/skipping
sl st(s) .... slip stitch(es)
sp(s) .... space(s)/spaced
st(s) .... stitch(es)
tog .... together
tr .... treble crochet
trtr ....triple treble
WS .... wrong side
yd(s) .... yard(s)
yo .... yarn over

YARN CONVERSION

OUNCES TO GRAMS		GRAMS TO OUNCES	
1	28.4	25	7/8
2	56.7	40	1 2/3
3	85.0	50	1 3/4
4	113.4	100	3 1/2

UNITED STATES		UNITED KINGDOM
sl st (slip stitch)	=	sc (single crochet)
sc (single crochet)	=	dc (double crochet)
hdc (half double crochet)	=	htr (half treble crochet)
dc (double crochet)	=	tr (treble crochet)
tr (treble crochet)	=	dtr (double treble crochet)
dtr (double treble crochet)	=	ttr (triple treble crochet)
skip	=	miss

Single crochet decrease (sc dec):
(Insert hook, yo, draw lp through) in each of the sts indicated, yo, draw through all lps on hook.

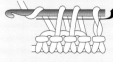

Example of 2-sc dec

Half double crochet decrease (hdc dec):
(Yo, insert hook, yo, draw lp through) in each of the sts indicated, yo, draw through all lps on hook.

Example of 2-hdc dec

Reverse single crochet (reverse sc):
Ch 1, sk first st, working from left to right, insert hook in next st from front to back, draw up lp on hook, yo and draw through both lps on hook.

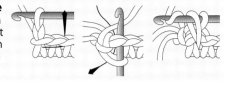

Chain (ch):
Yo, pull through lp on hook.

Single crochet (sc):
Insert hook in st, yo, pull through st, yo, pull through both lps on hook.

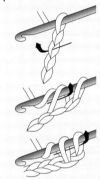

Double crochet (dc):
Yo, insert hook in st, yo, pull through st, [yo, pull through 2 lps] twice.

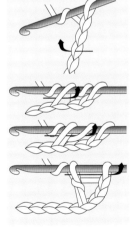

Double crochet decrease (dc dec):
(Yo, insert hook, yo, draw lp through, yo, draw through 2 lps on hook) in each of the sts indicated, yo, draw through all lps on hook.

Example of 2-dc dec

Front loop (front lp) Back loop (back lp)

Front Loop   Back Loop

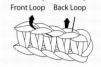

Front post stitch (fp): Back post stitch (bp):
When working post st, insert hook from right to left around post of st on previous row.

Back   Front

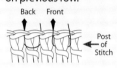

Post of Stitch

Half double crochet (hdc):
Yo, insert hook in st, yo, pull through st, yo, pull through all 3 lps on hook.

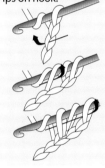

Double treble crochet (dtr):
Yo 3 times, insert hook in st, yo, pull through st, [yo, pull through 2 lps] 4 times.

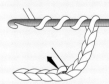

Treble crochet decrease (tr dec):
Holding back last lp of each st, tr in each of the sts indicated, yo, pull through all lps on hook.

Example of 2-tr dec

Slip stitch (sl st):
Insert hook in st, pull through both lps on hook.

Chain color change (ch color change)
Yo with new color, draw through last lp on hook.

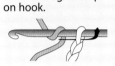

Double crochet color change (dc color change)
Drop first color, yo with new color, draw through last 2 lps of st.

Treble crochet (tr):
Yo twice, insert hook in st, yo, pull through st, [yo, pull through 2 lps] 3 times.

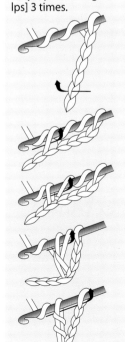

Annie's ™ *Wiggly Crochet Dishcloths* is published by Annie's, 306 East Parr Road, Berne, IN 46711. Printed in USA. Copyright © 2013 Annie's. All rights reserved. This publication may not be reproduced in part or in whole without written permission from the publisher.

RETAIL STORES: If you would like to carry this pattern book or any other Annie's publications, visit AnniesWSL.com

Every effort has been made to ensure that the instructions in this pattern book are complete and accurate. We cannot, however, take responsibility for human error, typographical mistakes or variations in individual work. Please visit AnniesCustomerCare.com to check for pattern updates.

ISBN: 978-1-59635-788-4

1 2 3 4 5 6 7 8 9